SEE NO...
HEAR NO...SPEAK NO...

MAD®

WARNER BOOKS

A Time Warner Company

Recently, a so-called "scary" movie (by Steven Spielberg et al) made box office history when millions of horror fans all around the country rushed to theaters and paid good money to have their pants scared off them. Well, Steve and Company, MAD has taken a long, hard look at your movie, and we've come to the conclusion that using a display of dazzling special effects to cover up the lack of a strong plot and the work of unknown actors is a pretty

PALTRY GUISE

ARTIST: JACK DAVIS   WRITER: ARNIE KOGEN

I'm **Heave Feeling**... a **modern suburban Father!** I make a **good living** and I've got a **comfortable home** and a **nice family!** But I'm a **little worried** about my **daughter, Caro Anne,** over there! She **stares at TELEVISION six hours a day!** That may not sound **strange** to you, but she stares at it **AFTER the shows have gone off the air!**
I'm **Dyin Feeling**... a **typical suburban housewife!** I'm **also** a typical **Steven Spielberg** suburban housewife! That could be a **problem!** They told me to **take** this role because being in a **Steven Spielberg movie** would mean **fame** and **recognition!** But after **this** movie, I'll **probably** be as **famous** as those **OTHER Spielberg housewives**... like **"Whatsername"** in **"Jaws"** and **"Whozit"** in **"Close Encounters"** and **"Watchacallit"** in **"E.T."!**
I'm **Blobbie Feeling!** I'm scared of the **big oak tree** outside! I'm scared of the **strange creaking noises** in the **attic!** I'm scared of the **glowing lights** in the **closet!** I'm **eight years old!** People ask me what I want to **BE** when I **grow up!** I tell 'em I want to be **NINE!** In **THIS** house, that **ain't** gonna be **EASY!!**
I'm **Tana Feeling!** I'm 16 years old! My **Mother** has **"Housewife-Career"** problems, my **Brother's** scared of **old trees,** my **Sister** talks to **TV sets** and I look **NOTHING** like **Brooke Shields!** I tell you, **PUBERTY is a drag!**
Are you **there?** Boy, talk about **GHOSTS** on your **TV screen!**
LA
TRANSYLVANIA TV

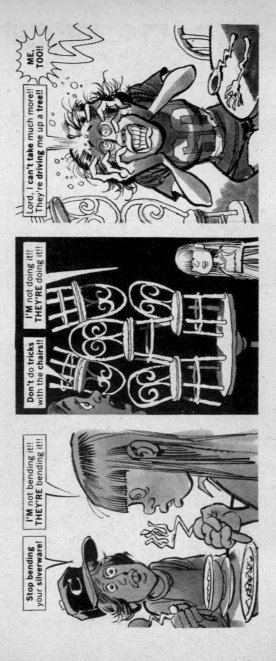

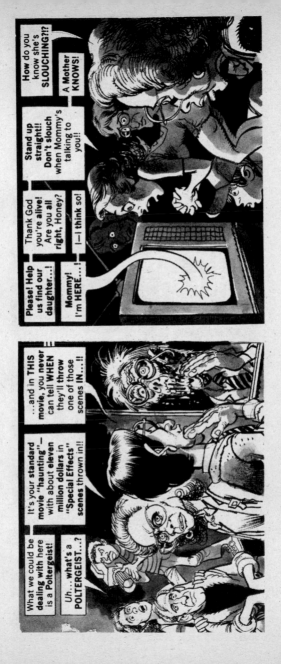

Boy, are you dumb! You've probably been shelling out good money to buy all the latest board games to entertain your friends. Well, we hate to tell you, but it's been a complete waste . . . because the most exciting new game around is played with a board and equipment that you can make yourself. And best of all, the fun can begin this very day . . . as MAD herewith presents the complete building plans and official playing rules for

THREE CORNERED PITNEY

ARTIST: JACK DAVIS   WRITER: TOM KOCH

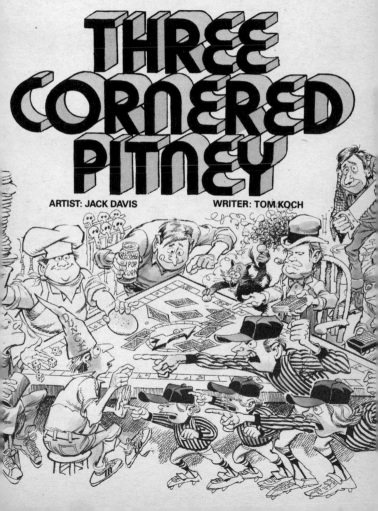

A Three Cornered Pitney board can be built in only a few hours from any scrap piece of inflexible material. (Inflexible means more like cast iron or lumber and less like feathers or chicken soup.) The most important thing to remember is to cut the board three cornered, since four cornered playing surfaces can only be used for such traditional games as Monopoly, Scrabble, tennis or polo.

Once your board is properly cut, mark off each of the three sides identically, except that one side should be left blank while the second should be divided into 23 green squares of equal size and the third should be covered with asphalt. (Asphalt is readily available in most areas. Look in the Yellow Pages under "Street Pavers".)

Place your completed Three Cornered Pitney board on top of any triangular card table. If you don't have a triangular card table, you can easily create two of them by sawing diagonally across a square card table, and then using either half (though the right half is preferred).

Major accessories needed to play the game can all be made from household odds and ends. The six wirtlings used in Three Cornered Pitney are merely golf balls with the centers hollowed out. The conch hacker (described below) may be fashioned from a yardstick cut down to the required 33½ inches. Finally, assembling the required set of 75 fox terrier skulls is easy, once you manage to locate a pet cemetery in your area that is going out of business.

Three Cornered Pitney is designed for any number of players, from two to nineteen, except eight. (This is because it never comes out even to deal a standard playing deck of 52 cards to eight people.) Each of the two-to-nineteen players should take a seat at a different corner of the triangular playing board. (This is another darned good reason why eight can't play and make it come out even.)

Before play begins, the deck of cards (mentioned above) should be placed in the center of the table face up, or, optionally, face down. Nearby, place the other objects to be used in the first round: one spinner, three dice, one can of popcorn (unpopped, of course), ten stacks of Susan B. Anthony dollars (to serve as chips) and 16 waffles (toasted, of course), that are to go in "The Widow".

Acting in unison, each player should draw one card from the deck, with the highest draw determining who gets to spin the spinner first to determine who gets to roll the dice first. If two players draw high cards of the same denomination, they shall settle the tie by seeing which one can hold their breath for the longest period of time.

If another tie results when spinning the spinner, the names of all the players with identical winning spins shall be written down on a slip of paper and mailed to an impartial observer out of town. While waiting for the impartial observers decision, go ahead and play the game.

Three Cornered Pitney officially begins when the first player rolls the three dice, and subtracts the number on one of them from the combined total shown on the other two. (Example: On a roll of 6-4-1, the 4 may be subtracted from the 6 + 1, or the 1 may be subtracted from the 6 + 4. The 6 may even be subtracted from the 4 + 1, but that leaves less than 0 and ends the game immediately.)

The player whose point total on the dice comes closest to the host's telephone number must announce the fact by calling out, "I vouchsafe that the opening vimmert has herewith elapsed." The others, realizing it takes only three vimmerts to make a complete farny, may respond by shouting either, "I challenge!" or "So's your old man"

Assuming there are no challenges, the first vimmert is declared finished, and the winner is entitled to eat one of the waffles that was placed in "The Widow" prior to the start of play. If the same player also picked the six of clubs on his opening card draw, he may add syrup to his waffle or, at his option, send out for a pizza.

Each of the other players shall remove one kernel from the can of unpopped popcorn, and use it as a marker to move up five spaces. This leaves everyone tied at the end of the opening vimmert, which makes for a good, close game and also prevents sore losers from getting violent.

To begin the second vimmert of the first farny, the host shall distribute the set of wirtlings, which you should know about by now because they've already been described adequately. Taking turns, each player must then roll his wirtling toward the kitchen door while quietly uttering the words, "I now roll my wirtling toward the kitchen." Any player who begins to giggle while doing this must immediately stand and move his marker back four spaces.

The shortest player is then picked to stand on his chair and deal the cards. This segment of Three Cornered Pitney is played exactly like Old Maid, except that one pair beats a straight flush, and spades are wild. Players who are dealt more red cards than black may move one space, while those who receive more black than red cards may go to the bathroom and stay there for as long as they like.

The player with the most average hand is declared the winner of the second vimmert, and collects one Susan B. Anthony dollar from each of the other players. He must then use his winnings to pay the toll charges for phoning a complete stranger in Honolulu to announce that he has just won the second vimmert. (Note: if the game is being played in Honolulu, phone a stranger in Cleveland.)

The player in fifth place after the second vimmert must use his conch hacker (described above) to strike the fox terrier skulls (described in the same place) until he has banged out a recognizable version of "Melancholy Baby." (During December, "Good King Wenceslas" may be substituted for "Melancholy Baby," but only with the written approval of two-thirds of the others playing the game.)

By previous arrangement, the family from next door shall then arrive to declare the official opening of the third vimmert. Most often, they are named Frank, Gladys and the twins. However, to comply with the rules of Three Cornered Pitney, they are designated Chief Honcho, Field Judge, Flight Attendant and First Lord of the Admiralty. For the remainder of the game, their decisions are final.

The player that is seated to the immediate right of the Field Judge begins the third vimmert of the first farny by proposing that all farnies, except the first one, be cancelled. This proposal is approved by a show of hands among the other players, whereupon the twins roll the wirtlings back from the kitchen while quietly uttering, "We now roll these wirtlings back from the kitchen."

The Chief Honcho is then free to state that the players have horsed around long enough and that, henceforth, the object of the game shall be to win it. He orders that each player shall roll the dice until one of them produces a combined total that will exactly carry his marker to the last of the 23 green squares (described above) on the hypotenuse of the Three Cornered Pitney board.

In response, the player with the highest I.Q. must rise to announce that he didn't understand that last instruction. This automatically obligates the Chief Honcho to restate that each player must roll the dice until one of them produces a combined total that will carry his marker to the last of the 23 green squares (described above) on the hypotenuse of the Three Cornered Pitney board.

Each player then rolls the dice and attempts to advance to the last square by means of cheating. There are several approved methods of cheating in Three Cornered Pitney. Examples: (1) Bounce the marker up and down in the same space while counting aloud to simulate movement; (2) Skip several spaces on each count to make the total come out right; (3) Roll 4 + 2 + 2 and cry out in a loud, clear and joyous voice, "Just what I needed—eleven!"

Any cheater who is klutzy enough to get caught may be ordered to gather up the waffles remaining in "The Widow" and reheat them in a microwave oven until they become black, hard and shrunken enough to be passed-off as hockey pucks to the first gullible Canadian clod passing by.

The successful players who were not caught cheating are all deemed to have finished in a tie for first place at the end of the closing vimmert. This situation requires the Flight Attendant to begin reading the rules for an overtime, which are purposely worded to be so dull that the players will leave in a group to go look for girls.

The host, after waiting for a mandatory period of three days, may then presume that the players are not coming back to finish the game, and act accordingly. Acting accordingly shall consist of officially declaring the final outcome of the game a tie, and forwarding news of this fact to the office of the National Three Cornered Pitney Association, which is currently closed for redecorating.

THE

SIDE

SCHOOL

LIGHTER OF...

ARTIST & WRITER:
DAVE BERG

SICKNESS

MARRIAGE

JOGGING

EATING

NEIGHBORS

EMPLOYMENT

PETS

TELEVISION

BUMPER STICKERS

PERSONALITIES

LOGIC

With **radio** and **TV signals** bouncing off **satellites** ...and **jet planes** and **bullet trains** and **fast automobiles,** the **world** is getting **smaller** and **smaller!**

So **how come** they keep **raising** the **price** of **POSTAGE STAMPS?!?**

OFFERS

SLEEP

When you see this sign, you know it means a slippery curve is ahead...

And when you see this sign, you know it means there's no smoking permitted!

Yessiree, all over the world, "picture signs" tell it like it is...without words or explanations...and people get their messages immediately! Which got us to wondering: Wouldn't it be great if this type of sign was used in even more places and situations? Then we'd be duly warned or informed by these—

PICTURE SIGNS FOR ALL OCCASIONS

ARTIST: BOB CLARKE   WRITER: FRANK JACOBS

OUTSIDE A TYPICAL SERVICE STATION...

HI·TEST

1. inept mechanic on duty.

2. Filthy restrooms.

3. Pumps may or may not contain grade of gasoline designated.

OUTSIDE AN EXCLUSIVE COUNTRY CLUB...

1. No Jews allowed.

2. No Blacks allowed.

3. No member of any kind of ethnic or minority group allowed.

OUTSIDE AN EXPENSIVE RESTAURANT...

1. Sky-high prices.
2. Slow service.
3. Very small portions.
4. No seating, unless Head Waiter is tipped.

OUTSIDE A NUCLEAR POWER PLANT...

1. High risk of radio-activity
2. ...as well as fallout
3. ...not to mention meltdowns.
4. Protestors keep out.

OUTSIDE A TOUGH NEIGHBORHOOD...

1. Stop for muggers.
2. Parked cars are stripped by residents.
3. Watch out for falling bodies.
4. Kiss your money goodbye

OUTSIDE A LATIN AMERICAN PRESIDENTIAL PALACE...

1. Assassination in progress.

2. Military take-over imminent.

3. Beware of Secret Police.

4. Bribe-taking as usual.

OUTSIDE A SWINGER'S APARTMENT...

1. Wild parties usually held

2. ...where marijuana is served

3. ...also cocaine.

4. No ugly broads admitted.

OUTSIDE A DOCTOR'S OFFICE...

1. Wait will be interminable.

2. Some painful injections are likely.

3. An accurate diagnosis is unlikely.

4. Doctor is into fee-splitting.

1. Deafening
   stereo.
2. Telephone
   tied up
3. Beware
   of messy
   clutter.
4. Obnoxious
   kid brother,
   stay out!

Who knows what a "Non Sequitur" is? Hands, please! Two...three...four! How soon you forget! Because it was just eight short years ago (July, 1974) that we explained what it is...when we ran an article called "Parental Non Sequiturs." Remember? Hands, please! Five... six... seven! Okay, we'll try again. You know how whenever you tell your parents something, no matter how important it is to you, it becomes nothing more than another opportunity for them to zap you with a criticism? Hands, please! Eight million...nine million...ten million! Well, when they do that, they're answering with a "Non Sequitur"—which is Latin for "It does not follow!"—and explains why Latin isn't spoken much any more. In other words, a "Non Sequitur" is something that's said... in response to something that's said...which doesn't make any sense. Like this stupid introduction! So read the article already! It's shorter, and you'll get the idea with:

MORE PARENTAL NON-SEQUITURS

ARTIST: PAUL COKER

WRITER: STAN HART

QUEUE TEASE DEPT.

A MAD LOOK AT LINES

ARTIST & WRITER: PAUL PETER PORGES

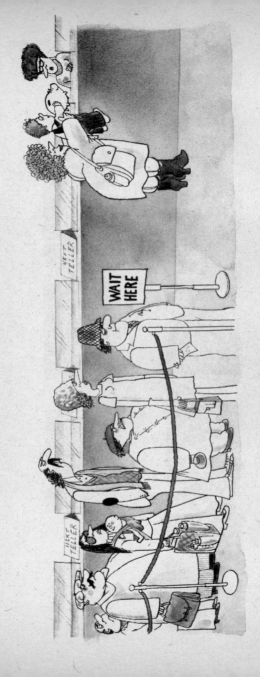

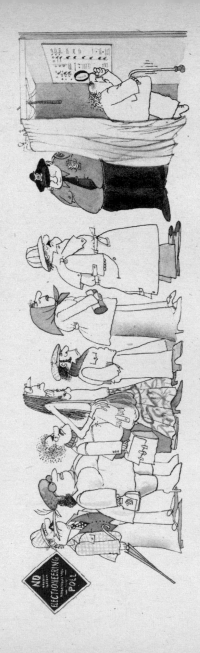

Have you ever noticed what happens to a TV situation comedy that's lucky enough to stay on the air beyond its opening season? The network "experts" immediately begin to tinker with its characters, its setting and even its basic premise in an effort to make sure the program has "something for everyone." In no time at all, the show becomes a total mish-mosh that includes "nothing for anyone." If you can remember the good old days when Archie Bunker still had a wife and a daughter and worked on a loading dock, or when Laverne and Shirley were brewery employees living in Milwaukee, then you're already familiar with the winding path that must be followed in this ridiculous article that studiously charts:

THE EVOLUTION OF A TV SITUATION COMEDY

ARTIST: HARRY NORTH   WRITER: TOM KOCH

THE FIRST SEASON

To the surprise of the network and the horror of many viewers, "Idle Hours" makes a successful debut. It is a nostalgic comedy about three high school chums (Nipsy, Conrad and The Horse) growing up in Kokomo, Indiana in 1946. Their idle hours are spent working as klutzy pin boys at a bowling alley which is owned by a retired clarinet player named Elsa. Also featured are the boy's gym teacher, Mr. Faunce, and Conrad's little sister, Buffy Lu. Buffy Lu is a typically American 14-year-old sexpot, whose smutty one-liners provide endless mirth.

THE SECOND SEASON

To avoid critics' charges that the show is too sugary, the network adds "social significance" by introducing The Horse's cousin, Mangler, as a new member of the cast. Mangler is a certified psychopath (but a funny one) who has chosen to hide in Kokomo following his escape from a southern chain gang. The leading characters try to rehabilitate him to a life of unending dullness by convincing him that he should enroll as an apprentice mortician at Kokomo's funeral home, which is operated by another new series regular, Mr. Ferndipper.

THE THIRD SEASON

The kid who played the role of The Horse quits the show to become a truly awful rock musician. The producers write him out of future scripts by saying he went to live in a leper colony. To take up the slack, Nipsy's little brother, Pooky, joins the cast as Elsa's new boy friend, despite a 35-year difference in their ages. Another element of hilarious romance is added as Mr. Ferndipper takes time out from his duties at the funeral home to begin courting Conrad's mother, a sassy, wisecracking widow who takes in laundry and drinks too much.

THE FOURTH SEASON

After portraying the high school seniors for three years, Nipsy and Conrad finally enter college, making it unrealistic for them to go on working as pin boys in a bowling alley. Therefore, Elsa trades her bowling alley for half interest in a sleazy poolroom operated by a hysterically funny Puerto Rican bigot named Emilio. This provides Nipsy and Conrad with a more adult hangout. It also provides the producers with a great chance to star the boy's former high school gym teacher, Mr. Faunce, in a new spinoff entitled, "The White Nebbish."

THE FIFTH SEASON

Following a fight in a tavern during the off-season, the actors playing Nipsy and Conrad both quit the show because neither will stoop to working with the other. To distract from their absence, the producers arrange for Pooky and Elsa to marry and adopt a Korean war orphan. Buffy Lu finally makes it to high school at 18, and finds Mr. Ferndipper teaching Freshman Embalming after turning over his funeral home to Mangler. Meantime, in a special Christmas Show, Emilio's 14 younger brothers and sisters arrive unexpectedly from Puerto Rico.

THE SIXTH SEASON

The program's creative planners become convinced that involving a tipsy midwestern widow with a lot of unruly children who don't speak English will make for a sure-fire comedy. Therefore, the new season is launched by having Conrad's mother opening a big rooming house for Emilio's younger brothers and sisters. While this brainstorm proves a total disaster, the network is nevertheless able to reap millions from its mistake by having Emilio and his family leave the show to star in a new spin-off entitled, "Fourteen Puerto Ricans Is Enough!"

THE SEVENTH SEASON

Elsa, left without a partner at the poolroom following Emilio's departure, is allowed to die of chalk dust inhalation. Pooky thus becomes a widower at 13, and is quietly dumped from the cast after giving the Korean war orphan to Conrad's mother and Mr. Ferndipper to raise. This naturally leads Mr. Ferndipper into asking Conrad's mother to marry him so the orphan won't think he's an illegitimate child. Their wedding is presented as a gala two-part episode that features Buffy Lu as the maid of honor and Mangler as mortician-in-waiting.

THE EIGHTH SEASON

Faced with the task of keeping a show alive that now stars an embalming teacher, his drunken wife and their Korean war orphan, the producers decide to move the setting from Kokomo, Indiana to Hollywood, California. This is logically explained by having Buffy Lu get a movie screen test offer that includes free lifetime lodging in California for all of her family and friends. The new locale permits the introduction of two wacky new series regulars, an unscrupulous talent agent named Marty and an untalented actor named Lance Surfshimmer.

THE NINTH SEASON

Seeking to capitalize fully on the new Hollywood setting, the show begins to feature such weekly guest ce-
lebrities as Annette Funicello and Conway Twitty. They
blend in the shows format by appearing as performers on
a small radio station that Mr. Ferndipper has bought
by borrowing on his life insurance. Meanwhile, Buffy Lu
and Lance Surfshimmer become co-stars of food chopper
demonstrations at supermarket openings, while Mangler
leaves the show to move into bachelor pad at the beach
and launch a new spin-off entitled, "One's Company."

THE TENTH SEASON

With the guest celebrity idea having fizzled, the network tries starring Marty, Mr. Ferndipper and Conrad's mother in a new show about life in a small radio station entitled, "KWRP In Anaheim." Buffy Lu and Lance Surfshimmer also depart to launch their own series about appliance demonstrators called, "One Supermarket Opening At A Time." This leaves no one on the orginal show except the Korean war orphan. When efforts fail to recast him as a 7-year-old truck driver with a pet ape, "Idle Hours" quietly goes off the air after 13 weeks.

LITTLE-KNOWN AND RARELY DIAGNOSED

AILMENTS

"THE CASH REGISTER TOTAL JAW DROP"

MAD

CONTRACTED AT...

SUPERMARKETS

ARTIST AND WRITER: DON EDWING

"THE CHECK CASHING ANXIETY ATTACK"

"FRIGID FREEZER FINGERS"

"PARKING LOT FOOT FATIGUE"

"THE SOAP AISLE SNEEZING ATTACK"

"AUTOMATIC DOOR CONTUSION"

"THE SPEEDING BASKET BASHED ANKLE"

"THE LONG LINE ANGER SPASMS"

"THE CHECK-OUT COUNTER CRUSHED HUSBAND"

THE BOOK OF ISTS DEPT.

As any psychiatrist worth his salt (or his $75 an hour) will tell you, we'd all be a lot better off if we viewed our lives, our expectations and our daily problems realistically. The trouble is that most of us don't do it that way. We're either overly optimistic and assume that everything will turn out all right, when it probably won't . . . or we're overly pessimistic and assume that everything will turn out all wrong, when some of it may actually turn out all right. Unfortunately, the most blissful optimists and the most gloomy pessimists are the last ones to realize that their view of the world is cockeyed. So, to straighten all you clods out, here's

A MAD LOOK AT THE DIFFERENCES BETWEEN OPTIMISM, & REALISM

PESSIMISM & REALISM

ARTIST: JACK DAVIS   WRITER: TOM KOCH

Upon hearing an insect buzzing around inside his moving car . . .

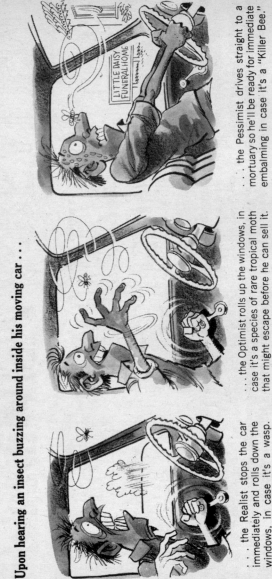

. . . the Realist stops the car immediately and rolls down the windows, in case it's a wasp.

. . . the Optimist rolls up the windows, in case it's a species of rare tropical moth that might escape before he can sell it.

. . . the Pessimist drives straight to a mortuary so he'll be ready for immediate embalming in case it's a "Killer Bee."

Upon being told by her date that she looks exactly like Cheryl Tiegs . . .

. . . the Realist knows exactly what the guy hopes to accomplish by telling her such lies, and accepts or rejects him.

. . . the Optimist takes the very next plane to New York City to seek fame and fortune as a professional model,

. . . the Pessimist worries that any kidnapper who may have plans to grab Cheryl Tiegs will get her by mistake.

Upon seeing the words, "For a good time, call Gertie at 555-8080" on a phone booth wall . . .

. . . the Realist knows this is some prankster's attempt to harrass an innocent girl.

. . . the Optimist showers and puts on a suit before calling the number, in case Gertie invites him to come right over.

. . . the Pessimist dutifully calls, even though he's sure that Gertie's a beast, and even more sure that she'll turn him down flat regardless.

Upon hearing a prolonged, high-pitched bleep broadcast over the radio . . . .

. . . the Realist figures it's just a Civil Defense test, and waits for regular programming to resume

. . . the Optimist figures it's the latest "punk rock" hit, and is overjoyed that he's one of the first to have heard it.

. . . the Pessimist figures it's an air raid alert, and spends the next month in a cellar waiting for the "all clear."

Upon being confronted by someone he knows while registering with a strange woman at a motel . . .

. . . the Pessimist gives his friend all the cash he has, and promises to make another blackmail payment in two weeks.

. . . the Optimist assumes that his friend is there with a strange woman too, and begins anticipating a group-fun evening.

. . . the Realist introduces her as his company's "Regional Manager" . . . and then hopes for the best.

Upon hearing that his plane can't take off until the morning because of the fog . . .

. . . the Realist is delighted the airline is concerned enough about safety to postpone the flight.

. . . the Optimist is delighted to have an opportunity to offer the Stewardess a place to stay overnight: his hotel room.

. . . the Pessimist is delighted to learn that his anticipated death in a plane crash has been put off for one more day.

Upon being mistakenly identified in a police line-up by a mugging victim . . .

. . . the Realist tries to think of someone who can vouch for his whereabouts at the time of the robbery.

. . . the Optimist gleefully anticipates being sent to prison, where he can finally get away from his nagging mother.

. . . the Pessimist doesn't even bother to get a lawyer, because he's sure he'll be lynched before his case comes to trial.

Upon seeing a long fly ball headed his way . . .

. . . the Realist knows . . . the Optimist is so sure he'll catch it . . . the Pessimist is so sure it's a homer, he he'll be traded if he and spark a winning streak, he begins plan- just hopes he won't break any bones crashing drops one more of these. ning how to spend his World Series check. into the wall in a futile attempt to catch it.

Upon seeing election returns that show a candidate he's trailing by twelve million votes . . .

. . . the Pessimist hires a bodyguard because he suddenly realizes he's even more unpopular than he thought.

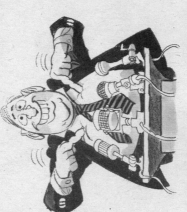

. . . the Optimist expects late returns from the West Coast to turn the tide because his nephew out there promised to vote for him.

. . . the Realist concedes defeat after blaming his loss on inflation and the civil war in El Salvador.

President Reagan wants to spend almost two trillion dollars on defense in the next few years. (We *spelled out* "two trillion" because we don't even know how many zeros there are in a trillion!) This news got us to wondering where all the money would be going. So we decided to check it out by assigning the one man really qualified to investigate this madness, MAD's top investigative reporter, Ed Razzner... who needs the work since he stopped playing Lou Grunt. Anyway, here's Ed's report on

MAD'S

"DEFENSE CONTRACTOR" OF THE YEAR

ARTIST: AL JAFFEE   WRITER: LOU SILVERSTONE

I still think half a million dollars is a lot of bread to spend on a a lousy portable latrine!
It's now a cool million, Ed! We've got to strip it down and re-design it for easy assembly... put it into a box... and print up instructions in English and Spanish!
Hey General how about a few extras like a plumber's helper and a reading lamp?
I love it!
How about a soft seat??
I never use anything else!
How about an "Officer's Model" with a hot tub??
Terrific!!
Hmm! Let's see! That'll come to two million bucks each!
As we say at the Pentagon, damn the costs... full speed ahead!
This is Ed Razzner, signing off for MAD Magazine!
Jaffee

There's scarcely an American kid who wasn't brought up on "Mother Goose." Now, MAD has found out that these rhymes are a favorite with kids in other countries, too! But the difference is that, somehow, the verses lose something in the translation. To show what we mean, take a "gander" at

MOTHER GOOSE AROUND THE WORLD

ARTIST: PAUL COKER   WRITER: FRANK JACOBS

IN SAUDI ARABIA...
Humpty Dumpty

Humpty Dumpty drilled a new well;
Humpty Dumpty leased it to Shell;
He's now worth a billion, this fortunate gent,
And entertains friends in his 20-room tent.

Humpty Dumpty lives like a king;
Humpty Dumpty knows a good thing;
And that's why each day he is thanking his stars
For people still driving those gas-guzzling cars.

IN FRANCE...
Mary Had a Small Cafe

Mary had a small cafe;
The meals she served were nice;
And ev'ryone who came agreed
She charged a modest price.

Mary's prices now are high;
How come? Well, here's the reason—
Today officially begins
A brand-new tourist season.

Peter, Peter

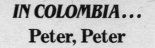

Peter, Peter, coffee grower,
Found his business getting slower;
Looked to make a greater gain,
Now makes a bundle from cocaine.

Peter, Peter, big supplier,
Sees his profits rising higher;
"Drugs are where it's at," he says;
"For coffee, go see Juan Valdez."

IN THE SOVIET UNION...
Wee Willie Winkie

Wee Willie Winkie
Conquers where he can;
Puts the screws to Poland;
Takes Afghanistan.

Wee Willie Winkie,
Always on the go,
Ships his guns to Cuba,
Arms the P.L.O.

Wee Willie Winkie
Loves to cause unrest;
Then, when war is starting,
Blames (who else?) the West.

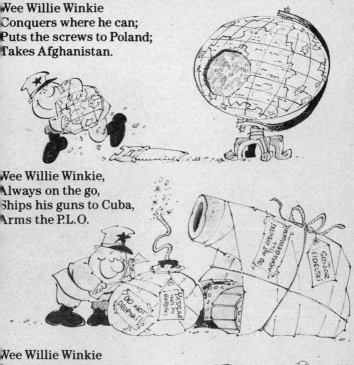

Sing a Song of Sonys

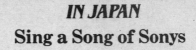

Sing a song of Sonys–
A pocketful of yen;
Magnavox and Zenith
Undersold again;
See the U.S. suffer
From the job we do;
This is how we get revenge
For losing World War II.

IN CENTRAL AMERICA...
Taffy Was a Strongman

Taffy was a strongman;
Taffy used his clout;
Taffy led an armed revolt
   and drove his rival out;
Taffy bled the country;
Taffy made a haul;
Taffy lasted 14 days,
   which isn't bad at all.

Old Mother Hubbard

Old Mother Hubbard
Went to the cupboard
To feed her poor doggie some buns;
She then filled his cup
With some water—poor pup!
He's been sick for a week with the runs.

IN ITALY
Little Miss Muffet

Little Miss Muffet
Got up from her tuffet
And made a big pot of linguini,
With baked canelloni
And sliced provolone,
Lasagna and veal scallopini.

Little Miss Muffet
Now plops on her tuffet,
Digesting the food that went in her;
She burped, then confided,
"I'm glad I decided
"To have a small snack before dinner."

IN THE MIDDLE EAST...
Solomon Grundy

Solomon Grundy
Arrived here on Monday,
Ducked bullets on Tuesday,
Took cover on Wednesday,
Was blasted on Thursday,
Assaulted on Friday,
Bombarded on Saturday,
Ambushed on Sunday;
So much for the peacekeeping
mission of Solomon Grundy.

A MAD LOOK AT

BIG-TIME TV

ARTIST & WRITER: PAUL PETER PORGES

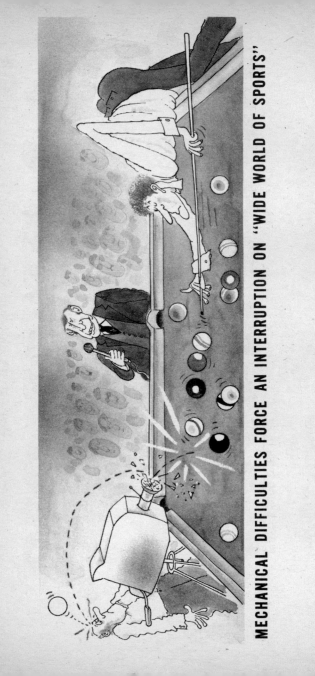

MECHANICAL DIFFICULTIES FORCE AN INTERRUPTION ON "WIDE WORLD OF SPORTS"

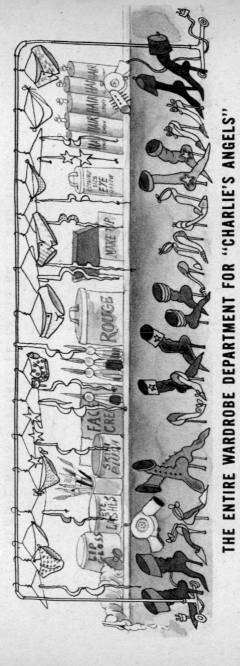

THE ENTIRE WARDROBE DEPARTMENT FOR "CHARLIE'S ANGELS"

REMOTE NEWS COVERAGE LOSES ITS AUDIO AND VIDEO

IMMEDIATELY AFTER THE SIGN-OFF ON "FAMILY FEUD"

"60 MINUTES" EXPOSING "20/20" EXPOSING "60 MINUTES" EXPOSING "20/20"...

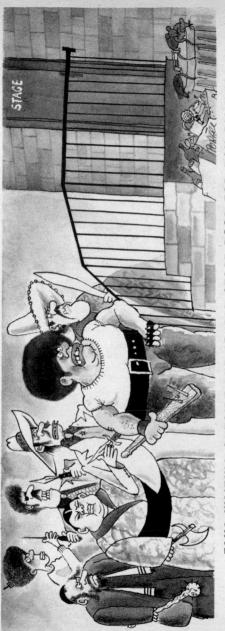

FANS WAITING OUTSIDE THE STUDIO STAGE DOOR FOR DON RICKLES

DURING A COMMERCIAL BREAK ON "THE JOHNNY CARSON SHOW"

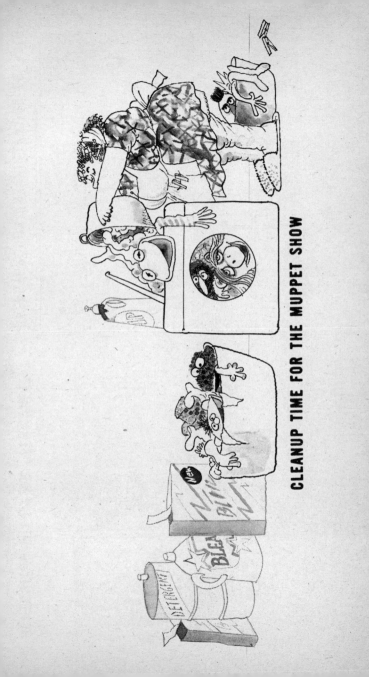

CLEANUP TIME FOR THE MUPPET SHOW

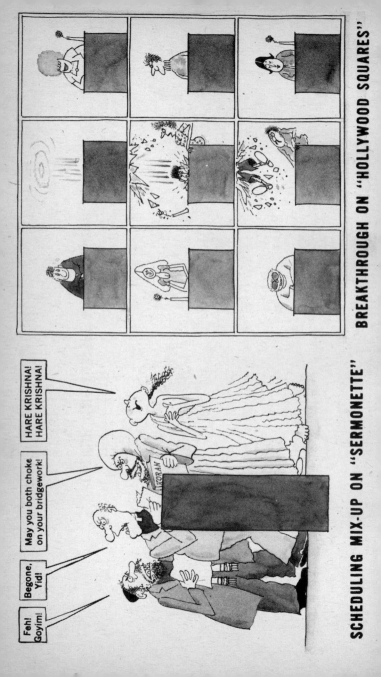

SCHEDULING MIX-UP ON "SERMONETTE"

BREAKTHROUGH ON "HOLLYWOOD SQUARES"

Wanna make a fast buck? Well, here's all you do: Take some cute little creature or popular movie hero, plaster his face on as many products as you can think of, and sell the hell out of him! This is called "merchandising", and it's making a fortune for a lot of smart promoters these days. Their items range from drinking mugs to bedspreads, from notebooks to knapsacks! And they're not finished with us yet! MAD feels that it's only a matter of time before these money-hungry promoters will be offering us the following assortment of . . .

MERCHAN- DISING

WE'RE ALMOST SURE TO SEE...AND HATE!

ARTIST: BOB CLARKE   WRITER: FRANK JACOBS

DRUG PRODUCTS...

HOME PRODUCTS...

DO-IT-YOURSELF PRODUCTS...

STRAWBERRY SHORTCAKE

"It's nice to be sure!"

HOME PREGNANCY TEST KIT

Easy To Follow Instructions Inside

A STRAWBERRY SHORTCAKE PRODUCT

RELIGIOUS ATTIRE...

AND, FINALLY,
FOR GOING
OUT IN STYLE...

There currently exists around the country specialized clusters of fervent fans who have formed clubs to pay tribute to their favorite cult heroes. We're talking about clubs like "The W.C. Fields Society", "The Baker Street Irregulars" (Sherlock Holmes fans), and "The Sons Of The Desert" (Laurel and Hardy addicts). These groups hold meetings, watch films, discuss trivia, collect memorabilia and engage in unique rituals saluting their idols (The Sons Of The Desert have an

LITTLE CELEBRITY GROUPS

annual pie throwing fight). Although the above mentioned clubs are the best known and have flourished for years, we've recently heard about some <u>other</u> little sub-culture groups popping up around the country. Each have their own tradition, requirements and rituals and each pays tribute, in their own special way, to other popular culture and media heroes. Who knows...you may find yourself wanting to join one of these......

KNOWN CULT

ARTIST: ANGELO TORRES

WRITER: ARNIE KOGEN

THE HELLO LARRY LEGIONNAIRES
(Cult Followers Of McLean Stevenson)

ENTRY REQUIREMENTS: Must have the personality of a shoe store clerk on uppers. Must worship and enshrine mediocrity, cheeseburgers, trailer parks, Ken Berry, Disney World, penny loafers, Sears lumber department and Robert Young commercials. Must not like or quite understand fettucini, New York Times editorials, Nureyev or Trini Lopez.

SECRET PASSWORD: Hi, how are ya? Really?... Well that's just great!

HANDSHAKE: Anything but a soul handshake.

ACTIVITIES: Members meet twice each year—on the first week of the new television season when McLean usually has a series—and four weeks later when the series is cancelled. The club flag (with the symbol "white bread over a pack of 'no doze' ") is raised and saluted. This is followed by a debate as to whether it was a right or wrong career move for McLean to quit M*A*S*H after only a few seasons. The same people then debate whether it was right or wrong for the Titanic to steer directly into the iceberg. The "Hello Larry Relief Fund" was established in June 1980. Underprivileged nations who don't have anaesthesia or medical supplies are sent the pilot film of "Hello Larry" Surgeons report that most patients fall into a deep sleep during McLean's first entrance.

THE ANNIE HALL MISFITS
(Cult Followers Of Woody Allen)

ENTRY REQUIREMENTS: Must be despondent. Must be in therapy. Must have hangups about sex, death, religion and having your pants altered without your knowledge.

SECRET PASSWORD: My grandmother was raped by Cossacks.

HANDSHAKE: Manic-depressive. Either totally ignoring the person you're supposed to be shaking hands with, or, using a novelty store joy buzzer.

ACTIVITIES: Meetings open with everyone chanting, "My one regret in life is that I am not someone else." This is followed by a hot lunch. After this, Woody's films are analyzed. His early funny films are compared to his later serious ones; his color films versus his black and white; Louise Lasser versus Diane Keaton and, mainly, what fears you experienced while sitting in the movie theatre. Field trips are taken to Brooklyn where members meet Woody's ex-teachers, the first haberdasher to sell him corduroy pants and the first bully to break his glasses. (This led to one of Woody's earliest lines, "The bigger they are, the greater the beating they're likely to give you.") Members then take subway rides home where they are mugged and sprayed with graffiti by cult followers of Charles Bronson.

CAUSE FOR DISMISSAL: Having a good time.

THE NOT-SO-NUTTY PROFESSORS
(Cult Followers Of Jerry Lewis)

ENTRY REQUIREMENTS: Must wear a pair of socks once and *only* once. Must be able to, in the space of a minute, go from being a nine-year-old clown to a grim, sullen, pompous adult. Must have I.Q. of 180 and an ego slightly bigger. Must wear a strange hairdo from no known period in our history.

SECRET PASSWORD: Mellman-Klevman-Lendl

HANDSHAKE: Handshake has been replaced with the French Legion Of Honor Kiss on both cheeks. (*Anything* French is worshipped in this club.)

ACTIVITIES: Members meet once a year at telethon time. In tribute to Jerry they stay up 24 hours without sleep. During this marathon they review (in English and French) Jerry's classic films. They applaud his development from the early 1960 films when he played a busboy and a Japanese General with buck teeth all the way to his current films where he plays a busboy and a Japanese General with buck teeth. Members then go into a verbal rampage about the state of the film industry, using four-letter words while decrying the lack of decent "family" pictures"

CAUSE FOR DISMISSAL: Failure to recognize French movie audiences and critics as the only knowledgeable people in the world.

THE I-DON'T-GET-NO-RESPECT SOCIETY
(Cult Followers Of Rodney Dangerfield)

ENTRY REQUIREMENTS: Must wear a tie. Must shrug and turn your head a lot, making it look like there's a coat hanger still in your jacket. Must look like you slept in your clothes. Must have had, on at least one occasion, the Surgeon General of the United States offer you a cigarette.

SECRET PASSWORD: I tell ya, my wife doesn't respect me. On Halloween she sends the kids out dressed like me!

HANDSHAKE: Sweaty.

ACTIVITIES: Club chapters are presently located in Jersey City, Three Mile Island, Mt. Saint Helen, an abandoned Chrysler factory, and Appalachia. Members meet on the 13th of every month and regale each other with stories about how they get no respect and have been mistreated. Veteran members ignore the person talking to them, causing them further despair and lack of confidence. Most chapters have a men's boutique that specializes in selling cheap blue suits and ill-fitting dress shirts. Meetings usually end when a stranger announces, "You people will have to leave, we want to start the 'Happy Hour'."

CAUSE FOR DISMISSAL: Getting even the slightest hint of respect from any person or thing on the face of the earth.

THE RENEE RICHARDS IRREGULARS
(Cult Followers Of Dr. Renee Richards)

ENTRY REQUIREMENTS: Must have either had a sex change operation, or are contemplating one, or, on at least one occasion, have been arrested for "propositioning yourself" in public.

SECRET PASSWORD: "Knock Knock" "Who are you?" "If I knew who I was would I be *here?*"

HANDSHAKE: Not quite limp-wristed yet not quite firm.

ACTIVITIES: The "Irregulars" have an annual country club bash in tribute to their idol and celebrating their new identities. The session opens with members singing "Hey, Look Me Over," followed by: A tennis tournament (mixed doubles), Self-help lectures ("I'm Okay, You're Okay, But The Guy In The Homburg Hat and Calico Dress Could Be In Trouble."), Medical films (Dr. Renee Richards "before" and "after"—there are no films of "during"), and climaxing with a gala dance. Prizes are awarded to members who continue to dance backwards without ever slipping back to their "former" selves and trying to lead.

CAUSE FOR DISMISSAL: Looking too much like a real woman.

THE SECOND BANANA JOLLYS
(Cult Followers Of Ed McMahon)

ENTRY REQUIREMENTS: Must be jolly, laugh heartily and be a good listener. Must be second in charge or an assistant with no chance of advancement to the top spot and *be able to live with this.*

SECRET PASSWORD: Heeeeeeeeere's (Fill in your name)…

HANDSHAKE: Fraudulently firm, warm and jolly.

ACTIVITIES: The first member to arrive at a meeting immediately goes and sits on the couch. As each new member enters, he gets up and moves one over. Then, one person gets up to tell about his day. The others laugh heartily at this, whether the stuff is funny or not. During the speech they interject with cries of "*How* hot was it?", "*How* cold was it?", "*How* crowded was the bus?" At the end of the evening six-packs of Bud are served. As the cans are shpritzed open, members laugh heartily at this.

CAUSE FOR DISMISSAL: Failure to laugh hearty.

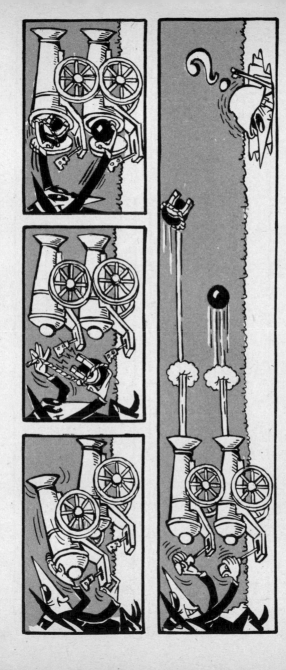

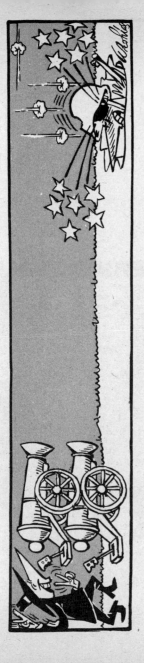

THE
SIDE

MODERN MORALITY

The **world** is getting **really rotten** these days! There's **no honesty left**! There are **no more scruples**! You **can't TRUST anybody** any more!!

This morning, somebody passed me some **funny money**... a **bogus bill**... a **counterfeit twenty**!!

LIGHTER
OF...

ARTIST & WRITER:
DAVE BERG

GROWING UP

RELATIONSHIPS

BABY SITTING

CONCLUSIONS

STATUS CLOTHING

SACRIFICES

ASSUMPTIONS

FIREMEN

COPS

WISDOM

NAGGING

ECONOMICS

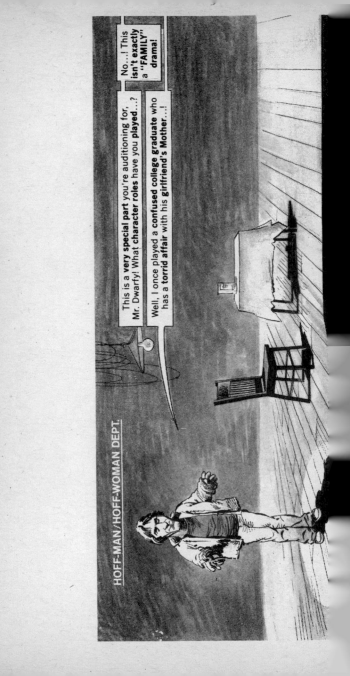